WORLD'S BEST
✳
RECIPES

Fish
& Seafood

Alexandre Libedinsky

Canadian Cataloguing in Publication Data

Libedinsky, Alexandre, 1963-

World's best fish and seafood
Translation of : Poissons et fruits de mer.
Includes index

ISBN 2-89535-019-1

1. Cookery (Fish). 2. Cookery (Seafood). I. Title. II. Series.

TX747.L5213 2001   641.6'92   C2001-940964-8

Design and layout:	Cyclone Design Communications Inc.
Photographs:	François Croteau
Translation:	Linda Arui
Revision:	Katrin Sermat
Proofreading:	Jane Jackel
Indexing:	Diane Baril

1 2 3 4 5   TOTAL 05 04 03 02 01

Éditions TOTAL Publishing
Outremont (Québec) Canada

Contents

Introduction

The first vertebrates to appear on earth were fish. Human beings came much later, but they were quick to realize that their aquatic forebears were a real treat! Our rivers, seas and oceans are home to thousands of species of freshwater, saltwater, bony, cartilaginous, tripod, flat and long fish.

We no longer have to travel hundreds of kilometres to find fresh fish. The corner fishmonger now offers exotic specimens from around the world. In fact, the very abundance of fish can sometimes be daunting. Although tempted by the variety of shapes and colours, we hesitate to take a chance, uncomfortable with the prospect of preparing a fish with which we are completely unfamiliar. FISH AND SEAFOOD, *World's Best Recipes*, will help broaden your culinary horizons and acquaint you with a selection of the world's best fish recipes.

While refrigeration and modern methods of transportation make it possible for us to enjoy the freshest fish every day, smoked, dried, pickled and fermented fish are still prized for their taste. Brandade, for example, owes its distinctive flavour to salt cod.

Generally much leaner than meat or poultry, fish is an excellent source of protein, phosphorus, magnesium, copper and iodine, as well as of vitamins A and D in the case of so-called fatty fish. And while we now know that our grandmothers were right when they told us that fish is "brain food" (because of its phosphorus content), studies have also shown that a regular intake of fish can considerably reduce the risk of cardiovascular disease.

FISH AND SEAFOOD, *World's Best Recipes*, presents a selection of the most exquisite fish dishes from around the world. These highly renowned and proven recipes are a delicious offering for any occasion, provided of course that the ingredients are fresh.

Shopping for fish

First, trust your nose: fresh fish smells like the sea and does not have the characteristic unpleasant odour of fish that has been on the shelf for days. Fresh fish will have clear, bulging eyes and bright scales, but buyer beware: fishmongers sometimes coat older fish with a mixture of egg white and water, which gives them a fresher look. The gills should be a bright, reddish pink and firmly attached to the body. Finally, the flesh should be moist and firm, not dried out.

Modern methods of preserving foods are generally quite effective, so that a fish that has travelled thousands of kilometres in a refrigerated cargo hold may be fresher than one that is sold a few feet from where it was caught. It all depends on the care the fisher takes to preserve his or her catch.

So now what? Do you prefer saltwater or freshwater fish? Do you like your fish poached, grilled, raw, fried or steamed? With hollandaise, wine or tomato sauce? Browse through the book and let yourself be tempted by thoughts of the sea. Both you and your guests will be delighted!

Soups and Coulis

15 mL olive oil 1 tbsp

2 medium onions, coarsely chopped 2

4 medium carrots, coarsely chopped 4

6 medium stalks celery, coarsely chopped 6

1 medium leek, coarsely chopped 1

2 medium potatoes, peeled and cut into pieces 2

1 can of diced tomatoes (796 mL/28 oz) 1

pinch saffron

10 mL dried basil 2 tsp

10 mL dried oregano 2 tsp

5 mL dried thyme 1 tsp

10 mL fennel seed 2 tsp

10 mL coriander seed 2 tsp

4 cloves garlic 4

2 bay leaves 2

pinch hot pepper flakes

2 kg fish trimmings (salmon, turbot, etc.),
rinsed and drained 4 lb

2 L water 8 cups

salt and freshly ground pepper

Rouille

15 mL olive oil 1 tbsp

30 mL tomato paste 2 tbsp

2 cloves garlic, chopped 2

pinch hot pepper flakes

pinch sugar

1 medium potato, peeled and well cooked 1

1 egg yolk 1

salt and freshly ground pepper

250 mL olive oil 1 cup

Fish Soup with Rouille

serves **6 to 8**

METHOD

1 In a large saucepan, heat the oil over moderate heat and sauté the vegetables and seasonings 4 to 5 minutes.

2 Add the fish trimmings and cook 2 to 3 minutes longer. Add the water and adjust the seasoning.

3 Bring to a boil, partially covered. Skim off any foam that forms on the surface and simmer 1 hour.

4 Purée in a blender, then strain.

5 Serve piping hot with the rouille.

ROUILLE

1 Heat 15 mL (1 tbsp) oil in a small frying pan over low heat. Add the tomato paste, garlic, hot pepper flakes and sugar and cook 4 to 5 minutes. Remove from heat.

2 Using a fork, mash the potato and blend into the tomato paste mixture. Strain into a bowl and let cool. Once the mixture has cooled, add the egg yolk and adjust the seasoning.

3 Using a wire whisk, beat in 250 mL (1 cup) olive oil one drop at a time, then in a fine stream, as if you were making mayonnaise.

4 Refrigerate until ready to serve.

5 Serve the soup with the rouille and cheese croutons.

Smoked Herring Coulis
serves **4 to 6**

INGREDIENTS

15 mL olive oil **1 tbsp**

1 medium onion, coarsely chopped **1**

125 g smoked herring fillets, cut into strips **1/4 lb**

1 clove garlic, chopped **1**

2 mL dried thyme **1/2 tsp**

1 bay leaf **1**

pinch cayenne pepper

freshly ground pepper

60 mL soy sauce **1/4 cup**

750 mL 35% cream **3 cups**

M ETHOD

1 Heat the olive oil in a medium-sized stockpot over moderate heat. Add the onion and cook 2 to 3 minutes. Add the herring, garlic and seasonings and cook 2 minutes longer.

2 Add the soy sauce, then the cream. Bring to a boil over low heat. Boil, uncovered, until reduced by half. Remove from heat.

3 Blend in a food processor or blender 2 to 3 minutes, or until smooth.

4 Strain and serve hot or cold.

Fish Consommé with Baby Scallops
serves **6 to 8**

INGREDIENTS

500 g white-fleshed fish, finely chopped **1 lb**

1 medium onion, cut into pieces **1**

2 large carrots, cut into pieces **2**

6 stalks celery, cut into pieces **6**

2 leeks, cut into pieces **2**

2 egg whites **2**

30 mL lemon juice **2 tbsp**

3 L cold fish stock **12 cups**

salt and freshly ground pepper

15 mL olive oil **1 tbsp**

15 mL butter **1 tbsp**

500 g baby scallops **1 lb**

60 mL chopped fresh parsley **1/4 cup**

M ETHOD

1 In a large saucepan, mix the fish, vegetables, egg whites and lemon juice with a wooden spoon.

2 Add the fish stock. Bring to a boil, stirring constantly, until a skin forms on the surface. Cook over very low heat 30 minutes.

3 Strain and keep hot. Adjust the seasoning.

4 In a large frying pan, heat the olive oil until very hot. Add the butter and sear the scallops 1 minute.

5 Drain the scallops on paper towels and lower into the hot broth.

6 Sprinkle with fresh parsley.

Crab Won Ton Soup

serves **6 to 8**

1 medium onion, cut into pieces 1

2 large carrots, cut into pieces 2

6 stalks celery, cut into pieces 6

1 leek, cut into pieces 1

125 mL white mushrooms,
cut into pieces 1/2 cup

4 cloves garlic 4

10 mL fennel seed 2 tsp

10 mL coriander seed 2 tsp

5 mL whole black peppercorns 1 tsp

5 mL dried thyme 1 tsp

4 bay leaves 4

pinch hot pepper flakes

15 mL olive oil 1 tbsp

3 L cold water 12 cups

2.5 kg live crabs 5 lb

Won tons

15 mL butter 1 tbsp

6 leeks, white part only,
finely chopped 6

chopped crab meat

2 cloves garlic 2

5 mL finely chopped fresh ginger 1 tsp

salt and pepper to taste

40 won ton wrappers 40

1 egg, beaten 1

water to cook the won tons

125 mL chopped green onions 1/2 cup

METHOD

1 In a large saucepan, sauté the vegetables, garlic and seasonings in the olive oil over moderate heat.

2 Add the water and bring to a boil. Reduce the heat to low and simmer, partially covered, 30 minutes.

3 Lower the crabs into the water. Return to a boil and simmer over low heat 8 to 10 minutes. Turn off the heat and let the crabs cool in the broth.

4 Remove the crabs and strain the broth. Refrigerate broth until ready to use.

5 Chop the crab meat and refrigerate until ready to use.

WON TONS

1 In a frying pan, heat the butter over moderate heat. Add the leeks and sauté 4 to 5 minutes.

2 Add the crab meat, garlic, ginger, salt and pepper and cook 2 minutes longer. Turn off heat and let cool.

3 To make the won tons, place 5 mL (1 tsp) crab mixture in the centre of each wrapper.

4 Lightly brush with beaten egg and firmly press the edges together.

5 In a large saucepan, bring the water to a boil and add the won tons. Cook uncovered 3 to 5 minutes, or until tender. Drain well.

6 In another saucepan, reheat the reserved crab broth and the won tons. Serve piping hot.

7 Sprinkle with green onions.

Cream of Broccoli and Mussels

serves **6 to 8**

INGREDIENTS

15 mL olive oil 1 tbsp
2 leeks, chopped 2
pinch dried thyme
2 bay leaves 2
pinch cayenne pepper
freshly ground pepper
1 kg mussels 2 lb
60 mL water 1/4 cup
1.5 L hot water 6 cups
salt and freshly ground pepper
2 medium heads broccoli, cut into florets 2
60 mL 35% cream 1/4 cup

M E T H O D

1 In a large stockpot, heat the olive oil over moderate heat. Sauté the leeks and seasonings, uncovered, 2 to 3 minutes.

2 Add the mussels and 60 mL (1/4 cup) water. Cover and cook 3 to 5 minutes, until the mussels open. Remove from heat.

3 Strain the liquid and pour it into a large saucepan containing 1.5 L (6 cups) hot water. Bring to a boil.

4 Adjust the seasoning and add the broccoli. Cook, uncovered, 2 to 3 minutes, so that the broccoli retains its colour.

5 Purée in a food processor or blender.

6 Add the cream. Heat 3 minutes, then add the shelled mussels. Reheat 1 minute without boiling. Serve piping hot.

Salmon Caldillo

serves **6 to 8**

INGREDIENTS

15 mL olive oil 1 tbsp
1 medium onion, thinly sliced 1
2 cloves garlic, chopped 2
1 can diced tomatoes (796 mL/28 oz) 1
1 mL dried thyme 1/4 tsp
2 bay leaves 2
2 L fish stock 8 cups
5 medium potatoes, peeled and cut into
2-cm (3/4-in.) slices 5
salt and freshly ground pepper
1 whole salmon, cut into steaks (2 kg/4 lb) 1
60 mL chopped fresh parsley 1/4 cup
60 mL chopped cilantro 1/4 cup

M E T H O D

1 In a large stockpot, heat the olive oil over moderate heat. Sauté the onion and garlic 2 to 3 minutes.

2 Add the undrained tomatoes, thyme, bay leaves and fish stock. Bring to a boil and simmer, partially covered, 4 to 5 minutes.

3 Add the potatoes, adjust the seasoning and cook 4 to 5 minutes longer, or until the potatoes are cooked but still firm.

4 Add the salmon steaks and cook 4 to 5 minutes. Do not overcook.

5 Serve piping hot with chopped parsley and cilantro.

Anchovy Butter
makes **500 g or 1 lb**

Tapenade
makes **500 g or 1 lb**

INGREDIENTS

500 g unsalted butter, cut into small cubes 1 lb

125 mL chopped fresh parsley 1/2 cup

2 cloves garlic, chopped 2

2 mL crushed black peppercorns 1/2 tsp

pinch cayenne pepper

30 mL lemon juice 2 tbsp

125 g anchovy fillets in oil,
drained and finely chopped 1/4 lb

INGREDIENTS

400 g black olives, pitted and drained 14 oz

125 mL capers 1/2 cup

3 cloves garlic 3

3 anchovy fillets in oil, drained 3

30 mL lemon juice 2 tbsp

pinch cayenne pepper

2 mL crushed black peppercorns 1/2 tsp

60 mL olive oil 1/4 cup

METHOD

1 Let butter stand in a large bowl at room
temperature 30 minutes.

2 Soften with a wooden spoon.

3 Add the remaining ingredients and mix well.

4 Wrap mixture in plastic wrap, shape into a roll
and refrigerate 2 hours.

METHOD

1 Purée all the ingredients in a food processor
3 to 5 minutes. Refrigerate until ready to serve.

2 The tapenade is at its best when prepared 2 days
in advance; it can be kept up to 2 weeks in the
refrigerator.

Shellfish Oil
makes **1 L or 4 cups**

1 L olive oil **4 cups**

1 kg crustacean shells (lobster, shrimp, etc.) **2 lb**

2 cloves garlic **2**

pinch hot pepper flakes

15 mL paprika **1 tbsp**

2 mL dried thyme **1/2 tsp**

2 mL whole black peppercorns **1/2 tsp**

2 bay leaves **2**

M E T H O D

1 In a saucepan, heat 30 mL (2 tbsp) olive oil over high heat. Add the shells and cook 3 to 5 minutes, or until they turn bright red.

2 Add the garlic, seasonings and the remaining oil. Reduce the heat to low and simmer, uncovered, 15 minutes.

3 Remove from heat, let cool and strain. Refrigerate.

4 Let stand at room temperature 1 hour before using.

Fish Stock
makes **2 L or 8 cups**

2 kg trimmings and bones of white-fleshed fish (whiting, burbot, turbot, etc.) **4 lb**

1 medium onion, cut into pieces **1**

1 large carrot, cut into pieces **1**

3 medium stalks celery, cut into pieces **3**

125 mL thinly sliced white mushrooms **1/2 cup**

4 cloves garlic **4**

10 mL fennel seed **2 tsp**

10 mL coriander seed **2 tsp**

2 mL whole white peppercorns **1/2 tsp**

5 mL dried thyme **1 tsp**

5 mL dried tarragon **1 tsp**

3 bay leaves **3**

2.5 L cold water **10 cups**

250 mL dry white wine **1 cup**

M E T H O D

1 Bring all the ingredients to a boil in a large stockpot.

2 Reduce the heat to very low and skim off any foam that forms on the surface. Simmer 20 minutes.

3 Strain and let cool.

4 The stock can be stored in the refrigerator for up to 4 days.

Cold Appetizers

Brandade

serves **4 to 6**

INGREDIENTS

1 kg salt cod **2 lb**
60 mL olive oil **1/4 cup**
250 mL 35% cream **1 cup**
2 mL ground white pepper **1/2 tsp**
pinch cayenne pepper
salt to taste
60 mL chopped fresh dill **1/4 cup**
250 mL Aioli **1 cup**

Aioli (makes 500 mL or 2 cups)

375 mL mayonnaise **1 1/2 cups**
125 mL plain yogurt **1/2 cup**
30 mL Dijon mustard **2 tbsp**
30 mL lemon juice **2 tbsp**
3 cloves garlic, chopped **3**
pinch cayenne pepper
salt and freshly ground pepper

METHOD

1 Place cod in a large bowl and cover with cold water. Let stand 12 hours, changing the water 6 to 8 times.

2 Remove the cod from the water and cut it into medium-sized pieces. Poach in hot water over very low heat 6 to 8 minutes.

3 Drain well. Remove the skin and bones, then shred the fish. Let stand at room temperature until ready to use.

4 In a large saucepan, heat the olive oil over high heat. Add the shredded cod and reduce the heat to low. Stir with a wooden spoon until a smooth paste forms.

5 Add the cream, pepper and cayenne pepper and mix well. Simmer 2 to 3 minutes over very low heat. Remove from heat. Stir in the salt and let cool. Stir in the dill.

6 Pour the brandade into a deep dish, cover with plastic wrap and refrigerate 12 hours.

AIOLI

1 Whisk together all the ingredients in a medium-sized bowl.

2 Refrigerate until ready to serve.

3 Serve the brandade hot with Aioli and croutons fried in oil.

Turbot Ceviche

serves **4 to 6**

INGREDIENTS

750 g fresh turbot fillets,
cut into 1-cm (1/2-in.) cubes **1 1/2 lb**

125 mL thinly sliced red onion **1/2 cup**

125 mL thinly sliced peppers
(red, green, orange, etc.) **1/2 cup**

1 clove garlic, chopped **1**

5 mL chopped jalapeño pepper (optional) **1 tsp**

125 mL lime juice **1/2 cup**

125 mL lemon juice **1/2 cup**

2 mL salt **1/2 tsp**

freshly ground pepper

60 mL chopped cilantro **1/4 cup**

60 mL chopped fresh parsley **1/4 cup**

60 mL olive oil **1/4 cup**

METHOD

1 Combine all the ingredients except the cilantro, parsley and oil in a large bowl. Mix well. Cover with plastic wrap and marinate in the refrigerator 5 to 10 minutes, or until the fish has lost some of its colour.

2 Add the cilantro and parsley. Mix well and serve.

3 Drizzle with olive oil.

Smoked Sturgeon Millefeuilles

serves **4 to 6**

20 sheets phyllo pastry **20**

125 mL melted butter **1/2 cup**

250 mL sour cream **1 cup**

60 mL chopped fresh parsley **1/4 cup**

60 mL chopped fresh tarragon **1/4 cup**

60 mL chopped fresh chervil **1/4 cup**

60 mL chopped fresh chives **1/4 cup**

pinch cayenne pepper

125 mL 35% cream **1/2 cup**

15 mL lemon juice **1 tbsp**

2 mL Dijon mustard **1/2 tsp**

salt and freshly ground pepper

500 g smoked sturgeon, sliced **1 lb**

METHOD

1 Preheat the oven to 190ºC (375ºF).

2 Cut the sheets of phyllo pastry in four. Brush each sheet with melted butter and layer them.

3 Cut an 8-cm (3-in.) circle from the layered sheets of pastry. Repeat with remaining sheets.

4 Place the circles of pastry on a baking sheet and bake 10 to 15 minutes, or until golden.

5 Remove from oven and let cool at room temperature.

6 In a large bowl, mix the sour cream, herbs and cayenne pepper. Refrigerate until ready to use.

7 For the sauce, beat together the cream, lemon juice and mustard. Adjust the seasoning. Refrigerate until ready to serve.

8 Place a circle of pastry on a work surface. Spread with sour cream mixture, cover with slices of sturgeon and top with another circle of pastry. Repeat twice more.

9 Arrange the millefeuilles on individual plates and surround with sauce.

Sardine Escabeche

serves **4 to 6**

INGREDIENTS

500 mL olive oil **2 cups**

1 kg fresh sardines, cleaned **2 lb**

4 medium carrots, cut into 1/2 cm (1/4-in.) slices **4**

4 medium onions, thinly sliced **4**

3 cloves garlic **3**

2 mL dried thyme **1/2 tsp**

2 mL dried rosemary **1/2 tsp**

4 bay leaves **4**

pinch hot pepper flakes

2 mL whole black peppercorns **1/2 tsp**

pinch salt

250 mL white wine vinegar **1 cup**

125 mL water **1/2 cup**

 METHOD

1 In a large frying pan, heat 250 mL (1 cup) olive oil over high heat and sear the sardines 1 to 2 minutes on each side. Remove from heat.

2 Place the sardines in a deep dish and let stand at room temperature.

3 Transfer the oil to a medium-sized stockpot. Add the vegetables, garlic and seasonings and cook over moderate heat 3 to 5 minutes.

4 Add the vinegar, water and the remaining oil and boil 15 minutes. Pour over sardines and let cool.

5 Refrigerate the sardines 24 hours before serving.

Bream Sashimi

serves **4 to 6**

INGREDIENTS

500 g bream fillets, cleaned **1 lb**

60 mL vegetable oil **1/4 cup**

15 mL sesame oil **1 tbsp**

30 mL rice vinegar **2 tbsp**

30 mL lemon juice **2 tbsp**

500 mL thinly sliced daikon radish **2 cups**

60 mL thinly sliced green onion **1/4 cup**

30 mL thinly sliced fresh ginger **2 tbsp**

salt and freshly ground pepper

30 mL black sesame seeds **2 tbsp**

METHOD

1 Cut the bream fillets into thin strips and arrange them around the edge of individual plates.

2 In a large bowl, whisk together all the liquid ingredients. Set aside 1/3 of the dressing.

3 Add the vegetables and ginger, adjust the seasoning and mix well.

4 Place the vegetables in the centre of the plates and drizzle the fillets with the remaining dressing. Sprinkle with sesame seeds.

Mussels with Salsa Verde

INGREDIENTS

15 mL olive oil **1 tbsp**

125 mL chopped celery **1/2 cup**

125 mL chopped onion **1/2 cup**

1 leek, white part only, chopped **1**

2 mL coriander seed **1/2 tsp**

1 mL whole white peppercorns **1/4 tsp**

1 mL dried thyme **1/4 tsp**

2 bay leaves **2**

1.5 kg mussels **3 lb**

60 mL white wine **1/4 cup**

cooking liquid from mussels

250 mL Salsa Verde **1 cup**

125 mL chopped fresh chives **1/2 cup**

Salsa Verde (makes 500 mL or 2 cups)

250 mL fresh parsley **1 cup**

60 mL cilantro **1/4 cup**

60 mL fresh dill **1/4 cup**

60 mL capers **1/4 cup**

60 mL green onion **1/4 cup**

2 cloves garlic **2**

30 mL lemon juice **2 tbsp**

15 mL Dijon mustard **1 tbsp**

1 mL salt **1/4 tsp**

freshly ground pepper

pinch cayenne pepper

125 mL olive oil **1/2 cup**

METHOD

MUSSELS

1 In a large stockpot, heat the olive oil over moderate heat and cook the vegetables and seasonings, uncovered, 3 to 5 minutes.

2 Add the mussels and the white wine. Cover and cook 3 to 5 minutes longer, or until the mussels open.

3 Shell the mussels, place them in a bowl and cover with strained cooking liquid. Refrigerate until ready to serve. Set aside half the shells.

4 To serve, drain the mussels of all but 60 mL (1/4 cup) of the cooking liquid and place them in a large bowl.

5 Add the Salsa Verde. Toss gently and place in shells.

6 Arrange the mussels on individual plates and sprinkle with chives.

SALSA VERDE

1 Purée all the ingredients in a food processor 3 to 5 minutes.

2 Refrigerate until ready to serve.

Smoked Salmon Rolls with Endives

serves **4 to 6**

INGREDIENTS

180 mL vegetable oil **3/4 cup**

45 mL sesame oil **3 tbsp**

15 mL rice vinegar **1 tbsp**

30 mL soy sauce **2 tbsp**

salt and freshly ground pepper

500 g endives, julienned **1 lb**

500 g smoked salmon, sliced **1 lb**

30 mL sesame seeds **2 tbsp**

METHOD

1 Whisk all the liquid ingredients together in a bowl. Stir in salt and pepper. Refrigerate until ready to use.

2 In a large bowl, toss the endives with half the dressing.

3 Place the salmon slices flat on a work surface. Place endives in the centre of each slice, letting them stick out 2.5 cm (1 in.) on either side. Roll the salmon around the endives and cut in two.

4 Place the rolls on individual plates and drizzle with the remaining dressing.

5 Sprinkle with sesame seeds.

Gravlax with Old-Fashioned Mustard

serves **4 to 6**

INGREDIENTS

750 g salmon fillet with skin **1 1/2 lb**
60 mL coarse salt **1/4 cup**
60 mL sugar **1/4 cup**
30 mL crushed black peppercorns **2 tbsp**
250 mL chopped fresh dill **1 cup**
1 medium lemon, sliced **1**
250 mL Old-Fashioned Mustard **1 cup**

Old-Fashioned Mustard
(makes 500 mL or 2 cups)
1 medium onion, chopped **1**
1 clove garlic **1**
30 mL balsamic vinegar **2 tbsp**
125 mL old-fashioned mustard (Meaux) **1/2 cup**
15 mL lemon juice **1 tbsp**
15 mL Worcestershire sauce **1 tbsp**
1 mL ground black pepper **1/4 tsp**
5 mL dried tarragon **1 tsp**
250 mL olive oil **1 cup**

METHOD

GRAVLAX

1 Place the salmon fillet in the centre of a sheet of aluminum foil, skin side down. Sprinkle with salt, sugar and pepper. Cover with dill and lemon slices. Wrap carefully and place in a deep dish.

2 Cover with a board. Place a weight (1 kg/2 lb maximum) on the board. Refrigerate 24 hours.

3 Remove the dill and the lemon slices.

4 Wipe the salmon carefully and serve in thin slices with Old-Fashioned Mustard.

OLD-FASHIONED MUSTARD

1 Blend all the ingredients in a food processor or blender until creamy.

2 Refrigerate until ready to serve.

Hot Appetizers

Scallops with Pickled Cucumbers

serves **4 to 6**

15 mL olive oil **1 tbsp**
15 mL unsalted butter **1 tbsp**
500 g large, fresh scallops **1 lb**
salt and freshly ground pepper
500 g Pickled Cucumbers **1 lb**

Pickled Cucumbers (makes 500 g or 1 lb)
5 medium cucumbers **5**
60 mL coarse salt **1/4 cup**
125 mL olive oil **1/2 cup**
30 mL balsamic vinegar **2 tbsp**
60 mL chopped fresh dill **1/4 cup**
salt and freshly ground pepper

METHOD

SCALLOPS

1 In a large frying pan, heat the olive oil over high heat. Add the butter and sear the scallops 1 minute on each side. Do not overcook. Sprinkle with salt and pepper.

2 Remove the scallops from the pan and arrange them on individual plates with warm Pickled Cucumbers.

PICKLED CUCUMBERS

1 Peel the cucumbers and cut them in half lengthwise. Using a small spoon, remove the seeds and slice into 1-cm (1/2-in.) half moons.

2 Place the cucumbers in a bowl, sprinkle with coarse salt and mix well. Let stand 30 minutes. Rinse with cold water, drain well and pat dry with paper towel.

3 Heat the olive oil over low heat in a 2-L (8-cup) saucepan. Add the cucumbers and simmer, uncovered, 10 to 15 minutes, or until pickled. Remove from heat.

4 Add the balsamic vinegar and the dill. Adjust the seasoning and let cool slightly before serving. Store in the refrigerator.

Frog Legs with Mushrooms

serves **4 to 6**

INGREDIENTS

30 mL olive oil **2 tbsp**

48 small frog legs **48**

500 g mixed mushrooms
(shiitake, oyster and portobello), thinly sliced **1 lb**

2 cloves garlic, chopped **2**

pinch cayenne pepper

salt and freshly ground pepper

30 mL white wine **2 tbsp**

180 mL 35% cream **3/4 cup**

60 mL unsalted butter **1/4 cup**

60 mL chopped fresh parsley **1/4 cup**

Marinade

30 mL olive oil **2 tbsp**

5 mL sesame oil **1 tsp**

15 mL soy sauce **1 tbsp**

5 mL Worcestershire sauce **1 tsp**

5 mL oyster sauce **1 tsp**

5 mL hoisin sauce **1 tsp**

2 mL paprika **1/2 tsp**

2 mL ground coriander **1/2 tsp**

2 cloves garlic, chopped **2**

pinch cayenne pepper

salt and freshly ground pepper

METHOD

MARINADE

Whisk all the ingredients together in a bowl. Add the frog legs and toss gently. Marinate in the refrigerator 2 hours.

1 In a large fry pan, heat half the olive oil over high heat. Sauté the frog legs 2 minutes.

2 Reduce the heat to moderate and cook 3 to 4 minutes longer, or until the meat pulls away easily from the bones. Remove from pan and keep warm.

3 In the same pan, heat the remaining olive oil and sauté the mushrooms, garlic and seasonings 2 to 3 minutes.

4 Deglaze with wine and add cream. Bring to a boil over high heat. Boil 1 minute.

5 Remove from heat and add butter gradually, stirring gently.

6 Place the sautéed mushrooms in the centre of individual plates, arrange the frog's legs around the edge and pour sauce over. Garnish with parsley.

Warm Oysters with Leeks

serves **4 to 6**

INGREDIENTS

36 fresh oysters **36**

15 mL unsalted butter **1 tbsp**

3 leeks, white part only, washed and finely chopped **3**

1 clove garlic, chopped **1**

pinch dried thyme

pinch cayenne pepper

freshly ground pepper

60 mL 35% cream **1/4 cup**

60 mL chopped chives **1/4 cup**

METHOD

1 Open the oysters and place them in a saucepan with their liquor. Strain and refrigerate until ready to use. Set aside the shells.

2 In a medium frying pan, melt the butter over moderate heat and sauté the leeks, garlic and seasonings 3 to 5 minutes.

3 Add the cream and cook 2 to 3 minutes longer.

4 Purée the mixture in a food processor. Keep warm.

5 Warm the oysters over low heat about 30 seconds. Drain well.

6 Divide the leek purée among the shells and top with the oysters.

7 Sprinkle with chopped chives.

Shrimp Quesadillas

serves **4 to 6**

12 20-cm (8-in.) wheat tortillas 12

500 g shredded mozzarella cheese **1 lb**

500 g small shrimp, cooked and shelled **1 lb**

250 mL thinly sliced peppers
(red, green, orange, etc.) **1 cup**

125 mL thinly sliced green onion **1/2 cup**

500 mL Salsa **2 cups**

250 mL sour cream **1 cup**

Salsa (makes 1 L or 4 cups)

1 can plum tomatoes (796 mL/28 oz) 1

3 cloves garlic 3

1 small jalapeño pepper, chopped (optional) 1

15 mL Worcestershire sauce **1 tbsp**

30 mL lime juice **2 tbsp**

125 mL chopped cilantro **1/2 cup**

125 mL chopped onion **1/2 cup**

125 mL chopped green pepper **1/2 cup**

10 mL ground cumin **2 tsp**

5 mL chili powder **1 tsp**

pinch sugar

salt and freshly ground pepper

METHOD

QUESADILLAS

1 Place half the tortillas flat on a work surface. Cover with half of the mozzarella cheese.

2 Mix the shrimp, peppers and green onions in a large bowl. Divide the mixture evenly among the tortillas.

3 Sprinkle the tortillas with the remaining mozzarella cheese and cover with the remaining tortillas. Refrigerate until ready to serve.

4 To serve, heat a non-stick frying pan over low heat. Cook the tortillas, one at a time, 2 to 3 minutes on each side. Remove from pan and cut into 6 pieces.

5 Serve hot with Salsa and sour cream.

SALSA

1 Purée all the ingredients in a food processor 3 to 5 minutes. Refrigerate until ready to serve.

Crab au Gratin

serves **4 to 6**

500 mL crumbled white bread, crust removed **2 cups**

250 mL milk **1 cup**

30 mL olive oil **2 tbsp**

1 medium onion, thinly sliced **1**

2 cloves garlic, chopped **2**

10 mL paprika **2 tsp**

2 mL dried thyme **1/2 tsp**

pinch cayenne pepper

750 g crab meat, cooked and shredded **1 1/2 lb**

250 mL fish stock **1 cup**

60 mL unsalted butter, cut into pieces **1/4 cup**

60 mL chopped fresh parsley **1/4 cup**

salt and freshly ground pepper

125 mL grated Parmesan cheese **1/2 cup**

METHOD

1 Soak the bread in the milk 30 minutes. Drain and squeeze out the liquid. Refrigerate until ready to use.

2 Heat the olive oil in a large frying pan over moderate heat and add the onion, garlic and seasonings. Cook 2 to 3 minutes.

3 Add the bread, crab meat and fish stock. Bring to a boil and turn off the heat. Stir in butter and parsley.

4 Adjust the seasoning and stir gently.

5 Place the mixture on individual plates or in crab shells, sprinkle with Parmesan cheese and broil 3 to 5 minutes, or until golden brown.

6 Serve piping hot.

Mixed Salads

Rollmops and New Potatoes with Aquavit

serves **4 to 6**

250 g salt pork, julienned **1/2 lb**

1 kg new potatoes, cooked but still firm **2 lb**

125 mL thinly sliced red onion **1/2 cup**

60 mL thinly sliced red pepper **1/4 cup**

60 mL thinly sliced green pepper **1/4 cup**

2 cloves garlic, chopped **2**

2 mL crushed fennel seed **1/2 tsp**

2 mL crushed cumin seed **1/2 tsp**

pinch cayenne pepper

salt and freshly ground pepper

250 mL Aquavit Dressing **1 cup**

750 g rollmops, drained* **1 1/2 lb**

60 mL chopped fresh parsley **1/4 cup**

Aquavit Dressing (Makes 250 mL or 1 cup)

15 mL aquavit **1 tbsp**

30 mL lemon juice **2 tbsp**

30 mL orange juice **2 tbsp**

60 mL olive oil **1/4 cup**

125 mL vegetable oil **1/2 cup**

2 mL Dijon mustard **1/2 tsp**

2 mL ground cumin **1/2 tsp**

2 mL ground fennel **1/2 tsp**

1/2 clove garlic, chopped **1/2**

pinch cayenne pepper

salt and freshly ground pepper

METHOD

1 Heat a large non-stick frying pan over moderate heat. Fry the salt pork until golden brown. Remove all but 15 mL (1 tbsp) fat from pan.

2 Cut the potatoes in half and sauté 3 to 5 minutes.

3 Add the red onion, peppers, garlic and seasonings and cook 2 to 3 minutes longer.

4 Place mixture in the centre of individual plates. Arrange the rollmops around the edge.

5 Drizzle with room-temperature dressing.

6 Sprinkle with parsley.

AQUAVIT DRESSING

1 Whisk all the ingredients together in a bowl. Refrigerate until ready to serve.

* Marinated herring fillets, rolled around a pickle or onion.

Trout Fillets with Blue Cheese

serves **4 to 6**

INGREDIENTS

15 mL olive oil **1 tbsp**

750 g trout fillets, cleaned, without the skin **1 1/2 lb**

250 g blue cheese, crumbled **1/2 lb**

freshly ground pepper

Watercress Salad

750 mL coarsely chopped watercress **3 cups**

60 mL julienned red pepper **1/4 cup**

60 mL julienned red onion **1/4 cup**

60 mL julienned carrots **1/4 cup**

250 mL Sesame Dressing **1 cup**

Sesame Dressing (makes 250 mL or 1 cup)

160 mL vegetable oil **2/3 cup**

30 mL sesame oil **2 tbsp**

60 mL rice vinegar **1/4 cup**

10 mL sugar **2 tsp**

salt and freshly ground pepper

METHOD

TROUT FILLETS WITH BLUE CHEESE

1 Preheat oven to 230°C (450°F).

2 Heat the olive oil in a large non-stick frying pan over high heat and sear the trout fillets 1 to 2 minutes on each side.

3 Remove from heat and place in an ovenproof dish.

4 Sprinkle with blue cheese and pepper and bake 1 to 2 minutes. Remove from oven and serve immediately over Watercress Salad.

5 Combine the watercress and vegetables in a salad bowl.

6 Add the Sesame Dressing. Toss well and serve.

SESAME DRESSING

1 Whisk all the ingredients together in a bowl. Refrigerate until ready to serve.

15 mL olive oil **1 tbsp**

60 mL coarsely chopped celery **1/4 cup**

125 mL coarsely chopped onion **1/2 cup**

1 leek, white part only, chopped **1**

1 mL coriander seed **1/4 tsp**

1 mL fennel seed **1/4 tsp**

pinch dried thyme

2 bay leaves **2**

10 mL curry powder **2 tsp**

salt and freshly ground pepper

1 kg mussels **2 lb**

60 mL coconut milk **1/4 cup**

60 mL 35% cream **1/4 cup**

250 mL flour **1 cup**

30 mL curry powder **2 tbsp**

15 mL paprika **1 tbsp**

10 mL garlic powder **2 tsp**

pinch cayenne pepper

2 mL salt **1/2 tsp**

freshly ground pepper

500 mL vegetable oil **2 cups**

30 mL chives **2 tbsp**

Kale Salad

1 kg kale, julienned **2 lb**

2 medium carrots, julienned **2**

250 mL Curried Mayonnaise **1 cup**

Curried Mayonnaise (makes 500 mL or 2 cups)

250 mL plain mayonnaise **1 cup**

125 mL plain 0.1% yogurt **1/2 cup**

125 mL sour cream **1/2 cup**

30 mL orange juice **2 tbsp**

reduced cooking liquid from mussels, cold

10 mL curry powder **2 tsp**

5 mL paprika **1 tsp**

2 mL Dijon mustard **1/2 tsp**

pinch cayenne pepper

salt and freshly ground pepper

Curried Mussels with Kale Salad

METHOD   serves **4 to 6**

1 Heat the olive oil in a large stockpot over moderate heat. Sauté the vegetables and seasonings, uncovered, 3 to 5 minutes.

2 Add the mussels, coconut milk and cream. Adjust the seasoning, cover and cook 3 to 5 minutes, or until the mussels open.

3 Shell the mussels and place them in a large bowl with half the strained cooking liquid. Refrigerate until ready to use.

4 In a small saucepan, bring the remaining cooking liquid to a boil. Boil 1 minute. Remove from heat and let cool. Refrigerate until ready to use.

5 Combine the flour, curry powder, paprika, garlic powder, cayenne pepper, salt and pepper in a medium-sized bowl.

6 Drain the mussels well and coat them with the flour mixture, shaking off the excess. Heat the vegetable oil in a frying pan until very hot (180°C/ 350°F). Lower the mussels into the oil a few at a time and cook 1 to 2 minutes.

7 Drain the mussels on paper towels and serve immediately with Kale Salad and the remaining Curried Mayonnaise.

8 Sprinkle with chives.

KALE SALAD

1 Combine the kale and the carrots in a salad bowl.

2 Add the Curried Mayonnaise. Mix well and refrigerate 1 hour.

CURRIED MAYONNAISE

1 Whisk all of the ingredients together in a bowl. Refrigerate until ready to serve.

Crab and Corn Croquettes

serves **4 to 6**

INGREDIENTS

500 g cooked crab meat, shredded **1 lb**

250 mL cooked corn **1 cup**

125 mL thinly sliced red pepper **1/2 cup**

2 cloves garlic, chopped **2**

5 mL Worcestershire sauce **1 tsp**

60 mL thinly sliced green onion **1/4 cup**

60 mL chopped cilantro **1/4 cup**

2 mL chili powder **1/2 tsp**

pinch cayenne pepper

125 mL bread crumbs **1/2 cup**

2 eggs **2**

salt and freshly ground pepper

30 mL olive oil **2 tbsp**

250 g baby spinach **1/2 lb**

375 mL Sun-dried Tomato Coulis **1 1/2 cups**

Sun-dried Tomato Coulis (makes 500 mL or 2 cups)

60 mL sun-dried tomatoes in oil, drained and coarsely chopped **1/4 cup**

5 mL paprika **1 tsp**

2 mL chili powder **1/2 tsp**

15 mL lemon juice **1 tbsp**

2 cloves garlic, chopped **2**

250 mL plain mayonnaise **1 cup**

250 mL plain yogurt **1 cup**

pinch cayenne pepper

salt and freshly ground pepper

METHOD

1 Blend together the crab meat, corn, red pepper, garlic, Worcestershire sauce, green onion, cilantro, chili powder and cayenne pepper in a large bowl. Add the bread crumbs, eggs, salt and pepper.

2 Shape the mixture into croquettes 2 cm (3/4 in.) thick. Refrigerate until ready to cook.

3 Heat the olive oil in a large frying pan over moderate heat and brown the croquettes 2 to 3 minutes on either side.

4 Remove from pan, drain on paper towels and serve piping hot with spinach and Sun-dried Tomato Coulis.

SUN-DRIED TOMATO COULIS

1 Blend all the ingredients in a food processor or blender until creamy. Refrigerate until ready to serve. For a thinner coulis, add a bit of cold water.

Fish Terrine with Baby Vegetables

serves **4 to 6**

INGREDIENTS

750 g white-fleshed fish, boned **1 1/2 lb**

180 mL 35% cream **3/4 cup**

2 egg whites **2**

15 mL olive oil **1 tbsp**

60 mL thinly sliced carrot **1/4 cup**

60 mL thinly sliced red pepper **1/4 cup**

1 leek, white part only, washed and thinly sliced **1**

1 clove garlic, chopped **1**

2 mL dried thyme **1/2 tsp**

5 mL dried tarragon **1 tsp**

1 mL ground white pepper **1/4 tsp**

pinch cayenne pepper

salt to taste

500 mL thinly sliced radicchio **2 cups**

250 mL Lemon Dressing **1 cup**

Lemon Dressing (makes 250 mL or 1 cup)

60 mL lemon juice **1/4 cup**

60 mL olive oil **1/4 cup**

125 mL vegetable oil **1/2 cup**

1 mL Dijon mustard **1/4 tsp**

1 mL dried basil **1/4 tsp**

1 clove garlic, chopped **1**

1 mL dried oregano **1/4 tsp**

pinch cayenne pepper

salt and freshly ground pepper

METHOD

1 Preheat oven to 180°C (350°F).

2 Blend the fish, cream and egg whites in a food processor until a smooth paste forms. Refrigerate until ready to use.

3 Heat the olive oil in a frying pan over moderate heat and sauté the vegetables, garlic and seasonings
3 to 5 minutes. Add salt and let cool.

4 Gently mix the fish paste and vegetables in a large bowl.

5 Line a 25 cm x 16 cm (10 in. x 6 in.) rectangular pan with two layers of plastic wrap. Pour mixture in the pan, place the pan in a larger pan of hot water and bake 45 minutes. Let cool before unmoulding.

6 Serve over radicchio and drizzle with Lemon Dressing.

LEMON DRESSING

1 Whisk all the ingredients together in a bowl. Refrigerate until ready to serve.

Warm Shrimp, Radish and Cucumber Salad

serves **4 to 6**

INGREDIENTS

45 mL olive oil **3 tbsp**

15 mL lemon juice **1 tbsp**

1 clove garlic, chopped **1**

1 mL dried thyme **1/4 tsp**

2 mL dried basil **1/2 tsp**

2 mL chili powder **1/2 tsp**

2 mL ground coriander **1/2 tsp**

pinch cayenne pepper

salt and freshly ground pepper

750 g large shrimp **1 1/2 lb**

3 medium English cucumbers, thinly sliced **3**

15 small radishes, thinly sliced **15**

250 mL Poppy Seed Dressing **1 cup**

Poppy Seed Dressing
(makes 250 mL or 1 cup)

125 mL olive oil **1/2 cup**

60 mL rice vinegar **1/4 cup**

15 mL sesame oil **1 tbsp**

15 mL lemon juice **1 tbsp**

15 mL poppy seeds **1 tbsp**

5 mL sugar **1 tsp**

salt and freshly ground pepper

METHOD

1 Mix together 30 mL (2 tbsp) olive oil, lemon juice, garlic and seasonings in a large bowl. Add the shrimp and marinate 1 hour in the refrigerator.

2 Heat the remaining olive oil in a large frying pan over high heat. Add the shrimp and sauté 2 to 3 minutes, or until cooked. Remove from pan and keep warm.

3 Combine the cucumber and radish slices in a salad bowl.

4 Pour half the dressing over the vegetables and mix well. Serve immediately on individual plates.

5 Top the vegetables with the warm shrimp and drizzle with the remaining dressing.

POPPY SEED DRESSING

1 Whisk all the ingredients together in a bowl. Refrigerate until ready to serve.

Vietnamese Marinated Squid

1 kg small squid, cleaned **2 lb**

10 mL sesame oil **2 tsp**

45 mL olive oil **3 tbsp**

15 mL lime juice **1 tbsp**

2 cloves garlic, chopped **2**

60 mL chopped lemon grass **1/4 cup**

10 mL fish sauce **2 tsp**

15 mL curry powder **1 tbsp**

pinch cayenne pepper

salt and freshly ground pepper

Salad

250 mL thinly sliced carrot **1 cup**

250 mL thinly sliced daikon radish **1 cup**

250 mL shredded Chinese lettuce **1 cup**

250 mL nappa (Chinese cabbage) **1 cup**

250 mL Vietnamese Dressing **1 cup**

Vietnamese Dressing

(makes 250 mL or 1 cup)

60 mL rice vinegar **1/4 cup**

30 mL fish sauce **2 tbsp**

180 mL coconut liquid **3/4 cup**

1 clove garlic, chopped **1**

1 mL fresh pepper paste **1/4 tsp**

5 mL sugar **1 tsp**

salt to taste

serves **4 to 6**

M ETHOD

SALAD

1 Cut the bodies and tentacles of the squid into 0.5-cm (1/4-in.) strips. Set aside a few whole tentacles for the garnish.

2 Place the squid in a large bowl. Add the sesame oil and 30 mL (2 tbsp) olive oil, lime juice, garlic, lemon grass, fish sauce and spices. Mix well and marinate 1 hour in the refrigerator.

3 Heat the remaining olive oil in a large frying pan over high heat. Sauté the squid 2 to 3 minutes. Do not overcook. Adjust the seasoning, remove from pan and keep warm.

4 Combine all the salad ingredients in a bowl. Pour 2/3 of the Vietnamese Dressing over the vegetables. Toss well and place in the centre of individual plates.

5 Arrange the squid around the edge and garnish with the whole tentacles.

6 Drizzle with the remaining dressing.

VIETNAMESE DRESSING

1 Whisk all the ingredients together in a bowl. Refrigerate until ready to serve.

Pan-Fried Scallops with Orange Fennel Remoulade

serves **4 to 6**

INGREDIENTS

30 mL olive oil **2 tbsp**
15 mL orange juice **1 tbsp**
1 clove garlic, chopped **1**
1 mL dried thyme **1/4 tsp**
2 mL paprika **1/2 tsp**
pinch cayenne pepper
500 g medium-sized scallops **1 lb**
salt and freshly ground pepper
375 mL Orange Mayonnaise **1 1/2 cups**
4 medium fennel bulbs **4**

Orange Mayonnaise
(makes 500 mL or 2 cups)
250 mL plain mayonnaise **1 cup**
125 mL plain 0.1% yogurt **1/2 cup**
80 mL orange juice **1/3 cup**
5 mL Dijon mustard **1 tsp**
30 mL old-fashioned mustard (Meaux) **2 tbsp**
1 clove garlic, chopped **1**
5 mL paprika **1 tsp**
1 mL ground white pepper **1/4 tsp**
pinch cayenne pepper
salt to taste

METHOD

1 Whisk together the olive oil, orange juice, garlic and seasonings in a bowl. Add the scallops, salt and pepper and toss gently. Refrigerate 1 hour.

2 Sear the scallops 1 to 2 minutes on each side in a large non-stick frying pan. Do not overcook. Remove from pan and keep warm.

3 Pour 250 mL (1 cup) of Orange Mayonnaise into a salad bowl.

4 Thinly slice the fennel using a mandoline or a sharp knife and place immediately in the salad bowl. Mix quickly to avoid oxidation. Serve the remoulade on individual plates.

5 Arrange the scallops around the edge and garnish with the remaining mayonnaise.

ORANGE MAYONNAISE

1 Blend all the ingredients together in a bowl. Refrigerate until ready to serve.

Seafood Sausage

serves **4 to 6**

500 g white-fleshed fish **1 lb**

2 egg whites **2**

125 mL 35% cream **1/2 cup**

125 mL coarsely chopped shelled shrimp **1/2 cup**

125 mL coarsely chopped scallops **1/2 cup**

30 mL olive oil **2 tbsp**

2 medium carrots, thinly sliced **2**

1 leek, white part only, washed
and finely chopped **1**

125 mL thinly sliced red pepper **1/2 cup**

60 mL thinly sliced green onion **1/4 cup**

2 cloves garlic, chopped **2**

2 mL dried thyme **1/2 tsp**

5 mL dried tarragon **1 tsp**

1 mL crushed black peppercorns **1/4 tsp**

pinch cayenne pepper

salt

2 L water **8 cups**

500 g mesclun **1 lb**

250 mL Lime Tamari Dressing **1 cup**

30 mL sesame seeds **2 tbsp**

Lime Tamari Dressing

(makes 250 mL or 1 cup)

180 mL olive oil **3/4 cup**

15 mL sesame oil **1 tbsp**

30 mL lime juice **2 tbsp**

30 mL tamari **2 tbsp**

1 clove garlic, chopped **1**

5 mL chopped fresh ginger **1 tsp**

1 Blend the fish, egg whites and cream in a food processor until a smooth paste forms. Place in a large bowl. Add the shrimp and scallops, mix well and refrigerate.

2 Heat 15 mL (1 tbsp) olive oil in a large frying pan over high heat and sauté the carrots, leek and red pepper 2 to 3 minutes. Add the green onion, garlic and seasonings. Stir in salt and cook 2 to 3 minutes longer over moderate heat. Remove from heat and let cool.

3 Gently blend the mixture with the fish and seafood paste.

4 Cover a work surface with plastic wrap. Using a piping bag, make sausages about 3 cm (1 1/4 in.) in diameter and 10 cm (4 in.) long. Wrap each sausage and tie the ends securely. Refrigerate.

5 Bring the water to a boil in a large saucepan and add the sausages. Reduce the heat to low and simmer, covered, 8 to 10 minutes. Remove from heat and let cool. Refrigerate.

6 To serve, heat the remaining olive oil in a frying pan and brown the sausages 2 to 3 minutes over low heat. Remove from pan and cut crosswise into 2.5-cm (1-in.) slices.

7 Place the mesclun on individual plates, garnish with sausage slices and drizzle with Lime Tamari Dressing.

8 Sprinkle with sesame seeds.

LIME TAMARI DRESSING

1 Whisk all the ingredients together in a bowl. Refrigerate until ready to serve.

Oyster, Pear and Zucchini Salad with Raspberry Dressing

serves **4 to 6**

INGREDIENTS

36 fresh oysters 36

250 mL Raspberry Dressing 1 cup

4 whole pears, washed 4

4 whole medium zucchini, washed 4

36 whole raspberries, washed 36

30 mL black sesame seeds 2 tbsp

Raspberry Dressing
(makes 250 mL or 1 cup)

125 mL olive oil 1/2 cup

60 mL walnut oil 1/4 cup

60 mL raspberry vinegar 1/4 cup

2 mL Dijon mustard 1/2 tsp

2 small shallots, chopped 2

1 clove garlic, chopped 1

2 mL dried tarragon 1/2 tsp

pinch cayenne pepper

salt and freshly ground pepper

METHOD

1 Open the oysters and place them in a bowl with their strained liquor. Refrigerate until ready to serve.

2 Pour the Raspberry Dressing into a salad bowl.

3 Using a mandoline or a sharp knife, cut the unpeeled pears into julienne strips and place them immediately in the salad bowl. Toss quickly to avoid oxidation. Cut the unpeeled zucchini into julienne strips and add to pear mixture.

4 Drain the oysters well and place them in the salad bowl. Toss gently and place the salad on individual plates.

5 Garnish with whole raspberries and black sesame seeds.

RASPBERRY DRESSING

1 Whisk all the ingredients together in a bowl. Refrigerate until ready to serve.

Main Courses

Salmon Sukiyaki

serves **4 to 6**

INGREDIENTS

750 g salmon fillet, without the skin **1 1/2 lb**
30 mL olive oil **2 tbsp**
500 mL julienned carrot **2 cups**
60 mL thinly sliced white mushrooms **1/4 cup**
60 mL julienned red pepper **1/4 cup**
60 mL julienned red onion **1/4 cup**
250 mL cooked vermicelli **1 cup**
2 mL dried basil **1/2 tsp**
1 mL fresh pepper paste **1/4 tsp**
1 clove garlic, chopped **1**
2 mL chopped fresh ginger **1/2 tsp**
pinch sugar
freshly ground pepper
125 mL soy sauce **1/2 cup**
45 mL sake **3 tbsp**
60 mL thinly sliced green onion **1/4 cup**

M ETHOD

1 Preheat oven to 240°C (475°F).

2 Cut the salmon into very thin strips (about 0.5 cm/1/4 in.) Refrigerate until ready to use.

3 Heat the olive oil in a large ovenproof frying pan over high heat and sauté the vegetables, vermicelli, basil, pepper paste, garlic, ginger, sugar and pepper 2 to 3 minutes. Remove from heat.

4 Top with the salmon strips and bake 1 to 2 minutes. Remove from oven and drizzle with soy sauce and sake. Sprinkle with green onion and serve immediately.

Pan-Fried Sea Bass with Carrots and Bok Choy

serves **4 to 6**

30 mL olive oil **2 tbsp**

1 kg sea bass fillet with skin, cut into 6 pieces **2 lb**

500 g carrots, thinly sliced **1 lb**

500 g bok choy, coarsely chopped **1 lb**

15 mL honey **1 tbsp**

15 mL rice vinegar **1 tbsp**

250 mL fish stock **1 cup**

15 mL soy sauce **1 tbsp**

salt and freshly ground pepper

60 g unsalted butter, cut into small pieces **1/4 cup**

METHOD

1 Heat 15 mL (1 tbsp) olive oil in a large frying pan over high heat and cook the bass 1 minute, skin side up. Turn over and cook skin side down over moderate heat 3 to 4 minutes longer, making sure the fish does not dry out. Remove from pan and keep warm.

2 Pour the remaining olive oil into the same pan and cook the carrots 2 to 3 minutes or until cooked but still firm. Add the bok choy and the honey and cook 1 minute longer.

3 Deglaze with rice vinegar, remove from pan and keep warm. Add the fish stock and soy sauce. Bring to a boil, adjust the seasoning and remove from heat.

4 Add the butter gradually, stirring gently.

5 Arrange the carrots and the bok choy on individual plates. Add the sea bass and drizzle with sauce.

Herbed Halibut with Broccoli Purée

serves **4 to 6**

INGREDIENTS

30 mL unsalted butter **2 tbsp**

1 medium onion, cut into pieces **1**

2 leeks, washed and coarsely chopped **2**

1 clove garlic, chopped **1**

1 mL dried thyme **1/4 tsp**

1 mL dried tarragon **1/4 tsp**

1 mL dried marjoram **1/4 tsp**

2 mL dried basil **1/2 tsp**

2 mL dried chervil **1/2 tsp**

1 mL coriander seed **1/4 tsp**

1 mL aniseed **1/4 tsp**

pinch cayenne pepper

250 mL fish stock **1 cup**

1 kg halibut fillets without the skin, cut into 6 pieces **2 lb**

salt and freshly ground pepper

250 mL 35% cream **1 cup**

3 L water **12 cups**

30 mL salt **2 tbsp**

2 medium heads broccoli, coarsely chopped **2**

60 mL walnut oil **1/4 cup**

60 mL chopped chives **1/4 cup**

1 Melt the butter in a large saucepan over moderate heat. Add the onion, leeks, garlic and seasonings. Cook 2 to 3 minutes.

2 Add the fish stock and bring to a boil.

3 Add the halibut to the saucepan with the salt and pepper. Cover and cook over low heat 3 to 5 minutes. Remove halibut from pan and keep warm.

4 Add cream to saucepan and bring to a boil. Reduce, uncovered, 2 to 3 minutes.

5 Blend in a food processor or blender 2 to 3 minutes. Strain and keep warm.

6 Bring the water to a boil in a large saucepan with 30 mL (2 tbsp) salt. Add the broccoli and cook, uncovered, 6 to 8 minutes, or until tender.

7 Drain well and purée in a food processor, adding the walnut oil gradually.

8 Place the broccoli purée on individual plates, top with the halibut, drizzle with sauce and sprinkle with chives.

Spicy Shrimp Risotto

serves **4 to 6**

INGREDIENTS

15 mL lemon juice **1 tbsp**

30 mL olive oil **2 tbsp**

15 mL Worcestershire sauce **1 tbsp**

2 cloves garlic, chopped **2**

5 mL chopped fresh ginger **1 tsp**

2 mL crushed coriander seed **1/2 tsp**

2 mL crushed fennel seed **1/2 tsp**

1 mL cardamom seeds **1/4 tsp**

5 mL curry powder **1 tsp**

1 mL fresh pepper paste **1/4 tsp**

30 whole shrimp **30**

salt and freshly ground pepper

30 mL unsalted butter **2 tbsp**

60 mL thinly sliced onion **1/4 cup**

60 mL thinly sliced red pepper **1/4 cup**

60 mL thinly sliced white mushrooms **1/4 cup**

2 pinches saffron threads **2**

375 mL arborio rice, rinsed and drained **1 1/2 cups**

750 mL fish stock **3 cups**

60 mL grated Parmesan cheese **1/4 cup**

60 mL Shellfish Oil (see page 19) **1/4 cup**

60 mL chopped fresh parsley **1/4 cup**

1 Whisk together the lemon juice, olive oil, Worcestershire sauce, garlic, ginger and seasonings in a large bowl. Add the shrimp, salt and pepper. Toss gently and marinate 1 hour in the refrigerator.

2 Cook the shrimp in a large non-stick frying pan over high heat 4 to 6 minutes, or until cooked. Remove from pan and keep warm.

3 Melt the butter in a medium-sized saucepan over low heat and cook the vegetables and saffron 2 to 3 minutes. Add the rice and cook 2 to 3 minutes longer.

4 Add the fish stock, adjust the seasoning and bring to a boil. Cover and cook over very low heat 20 minutes.

5 Remove from heat and add the Parmesan cheese, stirring gently.

6 Place the risotto on individual plates and top with the shrimp. Drizzle with Shellfish Oil and sprinkle with parsley.

Grilled Salmon Tournedos with Caper Butter

serves **4 to 6**

250 mL unsalted butter **1 cup**

125 mL chopped capers **1/2 cup**

60 mL chopped fresh parsley **1/4 cup**

1 clove garlic, chopped **1**

30 mL lemon juice **2 tbsp**

1 mL Tabasco sauce **1/4 tsp**

salt and freshly ground pepper

1.5 kg peeled potatoes **3 lb**

125 mL hot milk **1/2 cup**

125 mL finely sliced fresh sorrel leaves **1/2 cup**

1 kg salmon fillet cut into 6 tournedos **2 lb**

30 mL olive oil **2 tbsp**

60 mL fresh parsley **1/4 cup**

M E T H O D

1 Soften the butter in a bowl with a wooden spoon. Add the capers, parsley, garlic, lemon juice, Tabasco sauce, salt and pepper and mix well.

2 Place the caper butter on a sheet of plastic wrap and shape into a 2.5-cm (1-in.) roll. Refrigerate 6 hours.

3 Cut the potatoes into 2.5-cm (1-in.) cubes and cook in boiling salted water 15 minutes, or until cooked. Drain well and force through a potato ricer. Add the milk and sorrel, adjust the seasoning and keep warm.

4 Brush the tournedos with olive oil and sprinkle with salt and pepper.

5 Grill on a very hot barbecue 3 to 4 minutes on each side, or to taste.

6 Serve immediately with sorrel mashed potatoes and caper butter.

7 Garnish with fresh parsley.

Trout Fillets with Fresh Herbs

serves **4 to 6**

INGREDIENTS

60 mL chopped fresh tarragon **1/4 cup**

60 mL chopped fresh parsley **1/4 cup**

60 mL chopped fresh chervil **1/4 cup**

60 mL chopped fresh chives **1/4 cup**

1 kg trout fillets without the skin **2 lb**

30 mL Dijon mustard **2 tbsp**

salt and freshly ground pepper

30 mL olive oil **2 tbsp**

750 mL fettuccine, cooked al dente **3 cups**

60 mL white wine **1/4 cup**

2 small shallots, chopped **2**

250 mL fish stock **1 cup**

30 mL lemon juice **2 tbsp**

125 mL unsalted butter,
cut into small pieces **1/2 cup**

METHOD

1 Mix the fresh herbs in a small bowl and refrigerate until ready to use.

2 Brush the trout fillets with mustard and season with the chopped herbs, pressing the herbs gently into the fish.

3 Heat 15 mL (1 tbsp) olive oil in a large non-stick frying pan over high heat. Add the trout and cook 1 minute on each side. Remove from pan. Pour the remaining olive oil into the pan and sauté the fettuccine over moderate heat 3 to 5 minutes, or until piping hot. Keep warm.

4 Reduce the white wine and shallots by half in a medium-sized saucepan. Add the fish stock and the lemon juice. Reduce by half. Remove from heat and add the butter gradually, stirring gently. Adjust the seasoning. Keep warm.

5 Place the fish fillets on individual plates, add the pasta and drizzle with sauce.

6 Garnish with fresh herbs.

Snapper with Citrus Fruit and Polenta

serves **4 to 6**

INGREDIENTS

Polenta

1 L milk **4 cups**

salt and freshly ground pepper

250 mL cornmeal **1 cup**

60 mL unsalted butter **1/4 cup**

60 mL grated Parmesan cheese **1/4 cup**

60 mL chopped fresh rosemary **1/4 cup**

Fish and Dressing

3 medium oranges **3**

2 medium pink grapefruit **2**

3 clementines **3**

1 lime **1**

125 mL olive oil **1/2 cup**

1 kg snapper fillets, scaled **2 lb**

salt and freshly ground pepper

METHOD

POLENTA

1 Bring the milk to a boil in a 3-L (12-cup) stockpot. Stir in salt and pepper. Add the cornmeal gradually and cook over low heat 25 to 30 minutes, stirring constantly with a wooden spoon. Add the butter, Parmesan cheese and rosemary. Mix well and pour into a 25 cm x 10 cm (10 in. x 4 in.) pan lined with plastic wrap. Refrigerate 24 hours.

2 Cut the polenta into squares or diamonds and brown over moderate heat in a non-stick frying pan 2 to 3 minutes on each side.

FISH AND DRESSING

1 Over a bowl to catch the juice, use a knife to remove all the peel and white skin of the citrus fruits, so that the flesh is exposed.

2 Separate into sections and refrigerate with the juice until ready to use.

3 Heat 30 mL (2 tbsp) olive oil in a large frying pan over moderate heat and cook the snapper 3 to 5 minutes, skin side down. Remove from pan and keep warm. Pour the remaining olive oil into the same pan and warm over low heat. Add the fruit and the juice.

4 Add salt and pepper and beat vigorously. Heat 1 to 2 minutes without boiling. Remove from heat and keep warm.

5 Place the polenta and the snapper on individual plates and drizzle with the olive oil citrus dressing.

Sweet Scallops with Vegetable Chow Mein

serves **4 to 6**

INGREDIENTS

5 mL crushed fennel seed **1 tsp**

5 mL crushed coriander seed **1 tsp**

5 mL crushed aniseed **1 tsp**

5 mL crushed cardamom seeds **1 tsp**

5 mL crushed caraway seeds **1 tsp**

1 kg large, fresh scallops **2 lb**

15 mL olive oil **1 tbsp**

salt and freshly ground pepper

10 mL sesame oil **2 tsp**

60 mL thinly sliced red onion **1/4 cup**

60 mL thinly sliced red pepper **1/4 cup**

60 mL thinly sliced green pepper **1/4 cup**

60 mL thinly sliced carrot **1/4 cup**

60 mL thinly sliced broccoli **1/4 cup**

60 mL thinly sliced cauliflower **1/4 cup**

60 mL thinly sliced celery **1/4 cup**

750 g bean sprouts **1 1/2 lb**

15 mL hoisin sauce **1 tbsp**

30 mL oyster sauce **2 tbsp**

125 mL fish stock **1/2 cup**

30 mL sesame seeds **2 tbsp**

METHOD

1 Toast the spices in a small frying pan without oil over low heat 2 to 3 minutes, or until they release their aroma. Remove from heat, transfer to a large bowl and let cool.

2 Add the scallops and the olive oil. Mix well and marinate 1 hour in the refrigerator.

3 Sear the scallops in a large non-stick frying pan 1 minute on each side. Add salt and pepper. Remove from pan and keep warm. Add the sesame oil to the same pan and sauté all the vegetables except the bean sprouts over high heat 2 to 3 minutes.

4 Add the bean sprouts, hoisin sauce, oyster sauce and fish stock. Adjust the seasoning. Heat through, 1 to 2 minutes.

5 Remove from heat. Place the chow mein in the centre of individual plates. Arrange the scallops around the edge and sprinkle with sesame seeds.

Blue Marlin with Mango Salsa

serves **4 to 6**

INGREDIENTS

Marinade

125 mL hoisin sauce 1/2 cup

60 mL rice vinegar 1/4 cup

30 mL soy sauce 2 tbsp

10 mL Dijon mustard 2 tsp

5 mL chopped fresh ginger 1 tsp

1 clove garlic, chopped 1

1 pinch cayenne pepper 1

freshly ground pepper

1 kg blue marlin, cut into 6 pieces 2 lb

15 mL olive oil 1 tbsp

Mango Salsa

Mango Salsa

2 large mangoes, finely chopped 2

1 medium red onion, thinly sliced 1

125 mL finely chopped cilantro 1/2 cup

2 cloves garlic, chopped 2

30 mL sun-dried tomatoes in oil, drained and finely chopped 2 tbsp

30 mL rice vinegar 2 tbsp

15 mL olive oil 1 tbsp

10 mL brown sugar 2 tsp

pinch cayenne pepper

salt and freshly ground pepper

METHOD

MARINADE

1 Mix the hoisin sauce, rice vinegar, soy sauce, mustard, ginger, garlic, cayenne pepper and pepper together in a bowl. Add the marlin, cover with plastic wrap and marinate 6 hours in the refrigerator.

2 Remove the fish from the marinade. Refrigerate until ready to cook.

3 Heat the olive oil in a large non-stick frying pan over high heat and cook the fish 2 to 3 minutes on each side, or to taste.

4 Serve immediately on individual plates with Mango Salsa.

MANGO SALSA

1 Mix all the ingredients together in a large bowl and refrigerate at least 1 hour.

Grouper Fillets with Tomatoes and Black Olives

serves **4 to 6**

INGREDIENTS

15 mL olive oil **1 tbsp**

1 medium onion, thinly sliced **1**

2 cloves garlic, chopped **2**

1 mL dried thyme **1/4 tsp**

2 mL dried oregano **1/2 tsp**

2 mL dried basil **1/2 tsp**

1 mL paprika **1/4 tsp**

pinch cayenne pepper

125 mL pitted and chopped black olives **1/2 cup**

1 can diced tomatoes, drained (796 mL/28 oz) **1**

salt and freshly ground pepper

1 kg grouper fillets without the skin **2 lb**

125 mL chopped fresh parsley **1/2 cup**

Couscous

125 mL medium couscous **1 cup**

10 mL curry powder **2 tsp**

30 mL olive oil **2 tbsp**

250 mL hot water or vegetable broth **1 cup**

2 medium zucchini, diced **2**

1/2 clove garlic, chopped **1/2**

1 mL dried thyme **1/4 tsp**

METHOD

GROUPER

1 Heat the olive oil in a large frying pan over moderate heat and cook the onion, garlic and seasonings 2 to 3 minutes. Add the olives and tomatoes. Adjust the seasoning and cook
2 to 3 minutes longer.

2 Place the grouper fillets on top of the tomato mixture. Cover and cook 4 to 6 minutes. Do not overcook.

3 Serve immediately on individual plates with hot couscous. Sprinkle with fresh parsley.

COUSCOUS

1 Mix the couscous, curry powder and 15 mL (1 tbsp) olive oil in a large bowl. Add the hot water, adjust the seasoning and mix well. Cover with plastic wrap and let stand at room temperature 1 hour. Uncover and fluff the couscous with a fork. Refrigerate until ready to serve.

2 Heat the remaining olive oil in a medium-sized frying pan over high heat and sauté the zucchini, garlic and thyme 1 to 2 minutes. Adjust the seasoning. Remove from heat and let cool. Add the zucchini mixture to the couscous and reheat in the microwave before serving.

Surf and Turf Chowder

serves **4 to 6**

30 mL olive oil **2 tbsp**

500 g chicken thighs without the skin **1 lb**

125 g chorizo, thinly sliced **1/4 lb**

1 medium onion, thinly sliced **1**

2 cloves garlic, chopped **2**

1 mL dried thyme **1/4 tsp**

2 mL dried oregano **1/2 tsp**

2 bay leaves **2**

125 mL white wine **1/2 cup**

1/2 can diced tomatoes, drained (796 mL/28 oz) **1/2**

750 mL fish stock **3 cups**

36 fresh mussels, cleaned **36**

36 fresh clams, cleaned **36**

18 large shrimp, shelled **18**

60 mL chopped fresh parsley **1/4 cup**

60 mL chopped cilantro **1/4 cup**

60 mL thinly sliced green onion **1/4 cup**

1 Heat the olive oil in a large saucepan over high heat and brown the chicken 2 to 3 minutes. Add the chorizo, onion, garlic and seasonings and cook 2 to 3 minutes longer.

2 Deglaze with white wine.

3 Add the tomatoes and the fish stock and bring to a boil. Cover and cook over low heat 30 minutes, or until the chicken is no longer pink.

4 Add the mussels, clams and shrimp and cook, covered, 3 to 5 minutes longer.

5 Serve piping hot in deep dishes. Sprinkle with parsley, cilantro and green onions.

Skate Wings
with Watercress Coulis

serves **4 to 6**

INGREDIENTS

1.5 kg skate wings, with cartilage,
cut into 6 pieces **3 lb**

45 mL olive oil **3 tbsp**

15 mL lemon juice **1 tbsp**

salt and freshly ground pepper

2 L water **8 cups**

500 mL coarsely chopped watercress **2 cups**

30 mL salt **2 tbsp**

125 mL fish stock **1/2 cup**

375 mL 35% cream **1 1/2 cups**

30 mL unsalted butter **2 tbsp**

1 kg halved new potatoes, cooked but still firm **2 lb**

1 mL dried thyme **1/4 tsp**

2 mL dried oregano **1/2 tsp**

2 mL paprika **1/2 tsp**

METHOD

1 Place the skate in a large bowl and drizzle with olive oil and lemon juice. Add salt and pepper and toss well. Marinate 1 hour in the refrigerator.

WATERCRESS COULIS

1 Bring the water to a boil in a large saucepan. Add 30 mL (2 tbsp) salt and lower the watercress into the water 30 seconds. Remove and plunge into ice water. Drain well and refrigerate until ready to use.

2 Pour the fish stock and the cream into a saucepan and bring to a boil over low heat. Reduce by half, uncovered.

3 Add the watercress, adjust the seasoning and boil 1 minute. Remove from heat. Blend in a food processor or blender, then strain. Keep warm.

4 Heat a large non-stick frying pan and cook the skate 3 to 4 minutes on each side or until the flesh pulls away easily from the cartilage. Remove from pan and keep warm.

5 Melt the butter in the same pan and sauté the potatoes and seasonings 3 to 5 minutes, or until potatoes are golden brown. Keep warm.

6 To serve, cover individual plates with watercress coulis, top with the skate and surround with potato halves.

Mexican Pan-Fried Sea Bream

INGREDIENTS

30 mL olive oil 2 tbsp

15 mL lime juice 1 tbsp

1 clove garlic, chopped 1

2 mL ground cumin 1/2 tsp

2 mL chili powder 1/2 tsp

5 mL dried oregano 1 tsp

pinch cayenne pepper

salt and freshly ground pepper

1 kg sea bream fillets, scaled 2 lb

Jicama Salsa

60 mL cilantro 1/4 cup

Jicama Salsa

2 medium jicamas, cut into strips 2

1 medium red onion, thinly sliced 1

60 mL thinly sliced red pepper 1/4 cup

60 mL thinly sliced orange pepper 1/4 cup

60 mL thinly sliced green onion 1/4 cup

30 mL lime juice 2 tbsp

60 mL chopped cilantro 1/4 cup

60 mL chopped fresh mint 1/4 cup

5 mL chopped fresh ginger 1 tsp

15 mL olive oil 1 tbsp

10 mL brown sugar 2 tsp

1 small jalapeño pepper, thinly sliced (optional) 1

salt and freshly ground pepper

serves **4 to 6**

M E T H O D

1 Mix the olive oil, lime juice, garlic and seasonings in a bowl.

2 Brush the sea bream fillets with marinade and refrigerate 1 hour.

3 Heat a non-stick frying pan and cook the fish skin side down 2 to 3 minutes. Serve immediately with Jicama Salsa.

4 Garnish with cilantro.

JICAMA SALSA

1 Combine all the ingredients in a large bowl and refrigerate at least 1 hour.

Lobster Tails with Asparagus

serves **4 to 6**

3 L water **12 cups**

30 mL salt **2 tbsp**

1.5 kg lobster tails **3 lb**

30 mL olive oil **2 tbsp**

15 mL lemon juice **1 tbsp**

salt and freshly ground pepper

1 kg green asparagus, peeled **2 lb**

250 mL vegetable broth **1 cup**

30 mL unsalted butter **2 tbsp**

METHOD

1. Bring the water and salt to a boil in a large saucepan and add the lobster tails. After the water begins to boil once again, calculate 5 minutes and remove the tails. Let cool. Shell the tails and cut them into 1-cm (1/2-in.) slices.

2. Place the slices in a bowl and drizzle with olive oil and lemon juice. Sprinkle with salt and pepper and toss gently. Marinate 1 hour in the refrigerator.

3. Bring 3 L (12 cups) salted water to a boil in a large saucepan and add the asparagus. Cook for 7 to 8 minutes. Remove asparagus from saucepan and plunge into ice water. Drain and cut off 8-cm (3-in.) tips. Refrigerate until ready to use.

4. Bring the vegetable broth to a boil in a medium-sized saucepan. Add the asparagus and cook 1 minute.

5. Remove from heat, puree in a food processor or blender, then strain and reheat. Do not boil.

6. Turn off the heat and add the butter gradually, stirring gently. Adjust the seasoning. Keep warm.

7. Reheat the lobster and asparagus tips in a large non-stick frying pan over moderate heat 2 to 3 minutes.

8. Arrange on individual plates and drizzle with asparagus sauce.

Marinade

30 mL olive oil 2 tbsp

15 mL lemon juice 1 tbsp

2 mL paprika 1/2 tsp

2 mL dried basil 1/2 tsp

2 mL dried rosemary 1/2 tsp

1 clove garlic, chopped 1

pinch cayenne pepper

salt and freshly ground pepper

Fish

1 kg burbot fillets 2 lb

15 mL olive oil 1 tbsp

2 medium onions, thinly sliced 2

1 clove garlic, chopped 1

2 mL paprika 1/2 tsp

1 mL dried thyme 1/4 tsp

2 bay leaves 2

pinch cayenne pepper

pinch sugar

15 mL balsamic vinegar 1 tbsp

1 can diced tomatoes, drained
(796 mL/28 oz) 1

salt and freshly ground pepper

60 mL thinly sliced fresh basil 1/4 cup

Gremolata

Gremolata

30 mL bread crumbs 2 tbsp

30 mL fresh parsley 2 tbsp

2 cloves garlic 2

15 mL orange zest 1 tbsp

15 mL lemon zest 1 tbsp

pinch nutmeg

pinch cayenne pepper

salt and freshly ground pepper

Burbot Medallions with Stewed Tomatoes "alla Gremolata"

serves **4 to 6**

M E T H O D

1 Mix all the marinade ingredients together in a large bowl. Cut the burbot fillets into 2-cm (3/4-in.) medallions, toss with the marinade and refrigerate 1 hour.

2 Heat the olive oil in a large frying pan over high heat and cook the onion, garlic, seasonings and sugar 2 to 3 minutes, or until they begin to caramelize.

3 Deglaze with balsamic vinegar and add the tomatoes. Cook over moderate heat 4 to 5 minutes longer to eliminate the excess liquid. Adjust the seasoning and remove from heat. Add the fresh basil and keep warm.

4 Cook the burbot in a large non-stick frying pan over moderate heat 3 to 4 minutes without turning. Keep warm.

5 Place the stewed tomatoes on individual plates and arrange the burbot medallions around the edge, golden side up.

6 Sprinkle with Gremolata.

7 Drizzle with olive oil.

GREMOLATA

1 Finely chop the parsley and garlic and mix well with the remaining ingredients. Refrigerate until ready to serve.

Scampi Fricassee à la Marseillaise

serves **4 to 6**

INGREDIENTS

30 mL olive oil **2 tbsp**

36 large scampi, shelled **36**

60 mL Pastis **1/4 cup**

30 mL unsalted butter **2 tbsp**

2 shallots, finely chopped **2**

3 medium fennel bulbs **3**

1 clove garlic, chopped **1**

375 mL fish stock **1 1/2 cups**

125 mL 35% cream **1/2 cup**

salt and freshly ground pepper

60 mL seeded and chopped tomato **1/4 cup**

60 mL chopped fresh parsley **1/4 cup**

METHOD

1 Heat the olive oil in a large frying pan over high heat and sear the scampi 1 to 2 minutes.

2 Deglaze with Pastis and flambé. Remove scampi from pan and keep warm.

3 Add the butter, shallots, fennel and garlic to the same pan and cook over moderate heat 2 to 3 minutes. Add the fish stock and cream. Bring to a boil and reduce, uncovered, 1 to 2 minutes. Adjust the seasoning and remove from heat.

4 Garnish with tomatoes and parsley.

5 Serve immediately with scampi on individual plates.

Finger Food

Shrimp Tempura

serves **4 to 6**

INGREDIENTS

24 large shrimp 24
250 mL rice flour **1 cup**
125 mL cornstarch **1/2 cup**
5 mL curry powder **1 tsp**
2 mL ground coriander **1/2 tsp**
1 mL garlic powder **1/4 tsp**
2 mL onion powder **1/2 tsp**
1 mL ground white pepper **1/4 tsp**
pinch cayenne pepper
salt
250 mL lager **1 cup**
2 egg whites 2
1 L peanut oil **4 cups**
250 mL warm soy sauce **1 cup**

METHOD

1 Shell the shrimp, keeping the tails on. Refrigerate until ready to use.

2 Mix the rice flour, cornstarch and seasonings in a large bowl. Add enough beer to make a batter.

3 Beat the egg whites until stiff peaks form and gently fold into batter. Let stand at room temperature.

4 Heat the peanut oil in a 3-L (12-cup) saucepan over high heat to 180°C (350°F).

5 Hold the shrimp gently by the tail and dip in beer batter. Gently shake off excess batter and lower a few at a time into the hot oil. Cook 1 minute. Drain on paper towels. Serve immediately with warm soy sauce seasoned to taste.

Salmon Satay with Lemon Grass

serves **4 to 6**

INGREDIENTS

Marinade
500 g salmon fillets without the skin **1 lb**
5 mL fish sauce **1 tsp**
15 mL sesame oil **1 tbsp**
15 mL chopped lemon grass **1 tbsp**
5 mL lime juice **1 tsp**
2 cloves garlic, chopped 2
pinch cayenne pepper
salt and freshly ground pepper
Teriyaki Honey

Teriyaki Honey (makes 250 mL or 1 cup)
125 mL honey **1/2 cup**
60 mL soy sauce **1/4 cup**
60 mL orange juice **1/4 cup**
5 mL chopped fresh ginger **1 tsp**
pinch cayenne pepper

METHOD

1 Cut the salmon fillets into 2.5-cm (1-in.) cubes and combine with all the remaining ingredients except the Teriyaki Honey in a bowl. Marinate 1 hour in the refrigerator.

2 Heat a large non-stick frying pan over high heat and sear the salmon cubes 5 seconds on each side. Remove the cubes with toothpicks and arrange them on a large plate.

3 Drizzle with Teriyaki Honey.

TERIYAKI HONEY

1 Mix all the ingredients in a small saucepan and bring to a boil over very low heat. Turn off heat and let cool. Let stand at room temperature until ready to serve.

Sesame Tilapia Sticks

serves **4 to 6**

INGREDIENTS

500 g tilapia fillets without the skin **1 lb**

30 mL olive oil **2 tbsp**

15 mL lemon juice **1 tbsp**

2 cloves garlic, chopped **2**

pinch cayenne pepper

salt and freshly ground pepper

250 mL sesame seeds **1 cup**

Asian Ketchup

Asian Ketchup (makes 500 mL or 2 cups)

375 mL tomato ketchup **1 1/2 cups**

30 mL soy sauce **2 tbsp**

10 mL sesame oil **2 tsp**

15 mL rice vinegar **1 tbsp**

30 mL hoisin sauce **2 tbsp**

15 mL Worcestershire sauce **1 tbsp**

10 mL Dijon mustard **2 tsp**

10 mL chopped fresh ginger **2 tsp**

2 cloves garlic, chopped **2**

pinch cayenne pepper

salt and freshly ground pepper

METHOD

1 Cut the tilapia fillets into 6 cm x 2 cm (2.5 in. x 3/4 in.) strips and place them in a large bowl. Drizzle with olive oil and lemon juice. Add the garlic and cayenne pepper. Sprinkle with salt and pepper and marinate 1 hour in the refrigerator.

2 Place the sesame seeds on a baking sheet and roll the tilapia strips in them. Press the seeds gently into the fish. Refrigerate until ready to cook.

3 Heat a large non-stick frying pan over moderate heat and brown the strips 1 to 2 minutes on each side. Serve with Asian Ketchup.

ASIAN KETCHUP

1 Whisk all the ingredients together in a bowl. Refrigerate until ready to serve.

Mussel Guacamole

serves **4 to 6**

INGREDIENTS

15 mL olive oil **1 tbsp**
60 mL coarsely chopped celery **1/4 cup**
60 mL coarsely chopped onion **1/4 cup**
1 mL coriander seed **1/4 tsp**
1 mL fennel seed **1/4 tsp**
pinch hot pepper flakes
pinch dried thyme
freshly ground pepper
500 g mussels **1 lb**
60 mL white wine **1/4 cup**
guacamole
tortillas
2 limes **2**

Guacamole (makes 500 mL or 2 cups)
3 ripe avocados **3**
15 mL lemon juice **1 tbsp**
30 mL olive oil **2 tbsp**
125 mL seeded and chopped tomato **1/2 cup**
60 mL chopped green onion **1/4 cup**
2 cloves garlic, chopped **2**
1 jalapeño pepper, thinly sliced (optional) **1**
salt and freshly ground pepper

METHOD

1 Heat the olive oil in a large stockpot over moderate heat. Sauté the vegetables and seasonings 3 to 5 minutes, uncovered. Add the mussels and the white wine, cover and cook 3 to 5 minutes longer, or until the mussels open.

2 Shell the mussels, place them in a bowl, cover with strained cooking liquid and refrigerate until ready to serve.

3 To serve, drain the mussels well and mix gently with the guacamole.

4 Arrange the guacamole-covered mussels on a serving platter. Serve with tortillas and Mexican beer with lime.

GUACAMOLE

1 Using a fork, purée the avocados with the lemon juice and olive oil in a large bowl.

2 Add the remaining ingredients and refrigerate until ready to serve.

Anchovy Dumplings

serves **4 to 6**

30 mL olive oil **2 tbsp**

500 mL finely chopped onion **2 cups**

2 cloves garlic, chopped **2**

10 mL paprika **2 tsp**

1 mL crushed black peppercorns **1/4 tsp**

6 anchovy fillets in oil, drained and finely chopped **6**

125 mL chopped fresh parsley **1/2 cup**

40 won ton wrappers **40**

1 egg, beaten **1**

1 L peanut oil **4 cups**

250 mL Sour Cream and Wasabi **1 cup**

Sour Cream and Wasabi

250 mL sour cream **1 cup**

5 mL wasabi **1 tsp**

METHOD

1 Heat the olive oil in a large saucepan over low heat and cook the onions, garlic, paprika and peppercorns 3 to 5 minutes, covered, or until the onions are translucent. Add the anchovies and cook 1 to 2 minutes more, uncovered. Remove from heat and let cool. Add the chopped parsley.

2 Make dumplings by placing 5 mL (1 tsp) of the mixture in the centre of each won ton wrapper. Brush edges of wrapper lightly with beaten egg and press together firmly.

3 Heat the peanut oil in a 3-L (12-cup) saucepan over high heat to 180°C (350°F) and fry the dumplings, a few at a time, 1 to 2 minutes. Drain on paper towels.

4 Serve immediately with Sour Cream and Wasabi.

SOUR CREAM AND WASABI

1 Mix the ingredients together in a bowl and refrigerate. If you really like wasabi, you can double the amount.

Smoked Salmon Rolls

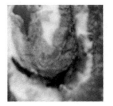

serves **4 to 6**

INGREDIENTS

125 mL cream cheese **1/2 cup**

60 mL chopped capers **1/4 cup**

60 mL chopped fresh parsley **1/4 cup**

60 mL chopped green onion **1/4 cup**

30 mL lemon juice **2 tbsp**

pinch cayenne pepper

freshly ground pepper

1 pkg nori **1 pkg**

250 g smoked salmon, sliced **1/2 lb**

Horseradish Whipped Cream

Horseradish Whipped Cream
(makes 250 mL or 1 cup)

250 ml 35% cream **1 cup**

15 mL grated horseradish **1 tbsp**

5 mL Dijon mustard **1 tsp**

salt and freshly ground pepper

METHOD

1 In a large bowl, beat the cream cheese with a wooden spoon 3 to 5 minutes, or until softened. Add the capers, parsley, green onion, lemon juice, cayenne pepper and pepper. Mix well. Let stand at room temperature until ready to use.

2 Place the nori flat on a work surface. Place slices of smoked salmon on top and cover with the cheese mixture. Roll into a cigar shape. Refrigerate 1 hour before serving.

3 Cut the rolls into 5-cm (2-in.) lengths and serve with Horseradish Whipped Cream.

HORSERADISH WHIPPED CREAM

1 Whip the cream over an ice-filled container. Add the horseradish, mustard, salt and pepper and mix well. Refrigerate until ready to serve.

Fish Chimichangas

serves **4 to 6**

INGREDIENTS

500 g white-fleshed fish
(turbot, sole, etc.), boned **1 lb**

60 mL 35% cream **1/4 cup**

1 egg white **1**

15 mL lemon juice **1 tbsp**

1 mL ground cumin **1/4 tsp**

2 mL chili powder **1/2 tsp**

pinch of cayenne pepper

salt and freshly ground pepper

18 14-cm (5.5-in.) corn tortillas **18**

1 L peanut oil **4 cups**

Salsa (see Shrimp Quesadillas, see p. 45)

METHOD

1 Blend the fish, cream, egg white, lemon juice and seasonings in a food processor until a smooth paste forms.

2 Place equal amounts of paste in the centre of each tortilla and roll into a small cigar. Pin the ends together with toothpicks and fry in very hot oil (180°C / 350°F), a few at a time, 1 to 2 minutes. Drain on paper towels.

3 Serve piping hot with salsa.

Littleneck Clams with Lemon

serves **4 to 6**

INGREDIENTS

60 fresh littleneck clams **60**

250 mL lemon juice **1 cup**

pinch of cayenne pepper

freshly ground pepper

60 mL chopped fresh parsley **1/4 cup**

METHOD

1 Thoroughly clean the clams in cold water and open them, keeping the flesh in one half-shell. Using a small knife, sever the muscle connecting the clam to the shell.

2 Mix together the lemon juice, cayenne pepper, pepper and parsley. Drizzle the clams with juice. Discard any that do not move. The success of this dish relies on the freshness of the clams.

Scallops Parmesan

serves **4 to 6**

INGREDIENTS

30 medium-sized fresh scallops 30

125 mL unsalted butter 1/2 cup

60 mL white wine 1/4 cup

60 mL fish stock 1/4 cup

freshly ground pepper

125 mL fresh Parmesan cheese, grated 1/2 cup

2 lemons, quartered 2

60 mL fresh parsley 1/4 cup

M E T H O D

1 Preheat oven to 230°C (450°F).

2 Place scallops in small shells or snail plates. Add a small piece of butter and drizzle with white wine and fish stock. Sprinkle with pepper and Parmesan cheese.

3 Bake 1 to 2 minutes.

4 Garnish with lemon quarters and fresh parsley.

Snails with Bacon

serves **4 to 6**

INGREDIENTS

30 mL olive oil 2 tbsp

48 small snails, rinsed and drained 48

2 cloves garlic, chopped 2

1 mL dried thyme 1/4 tsp

2 mL paprika 1/2 tsp

pinch cayenne pepper

freshly ground pepper

16 strips pre-cooked bacon 16

60 mL chopped fresh parsley 1/4 cup

M E T H O D

1 Heat the olive oil in a large frying pan over high heat and sauté the snails, garlic and seasonings 2 to 3 minutes. Remove from heat and let cool.

2 Cut the slices of bacon crosswise into three pieces. Roll a small slice of bacon around each snail and arrange on skewers. Refrigerate until ready to cook.

3 Heat a large non-stick frying pan over moderate heat and brown the snail and bacon brochettes 2 to 3 minutes. Drain on paper towels and serve immediately.

4 Sprinkle with chopped parsley.

Turbot and Chorizo Brochettes

serves **4 to 6**

INGREDIENTS

375 g turbot fillets 3/4 lb

15 mL olive oil 1 tbsp

15 mL lemon juice 1 tbsp

2 mL dried oregano 1/2 tsp

pinch cayenne pepper

freshly ground pepper

125 g chorizo (dry Spanish sausage),
thinly sliced 1/4 lb

60 mL Shellfish Oil (see page 19) 1/4 cup

60 mL cilantro 1/4 cup

M E T H O D

1 Cut the turbot fillets into 6 cm x 1 cm
(2.5 in. x 1/2 in.) strips and place in a bowl.
Drizzle with olive oil and lemon juice. Add the
seasonings, mix well and marinate 1 hour in
the refrigerator.

2 Fold each piece of turbot in two and place a
piece of chorizo in the middle. Fasten with a
toothpick and refrigerate until ready to cook.

3 Heat a large non-stick frying pan over high
heat and brown 20 seconds on each side.

4 Serve with Shellfish Oil and cilantro.

Shrimp Treats

makes **12**

INGREDIENTS

15 mL olive oil 1 tbsp

60 mL thinly sliced onion 1/4 cup

1 clove garlic, chopped 1

5 mL paprika 1 tsp

2 mL dried thyme 1/2 tsp

pinch cayenne pepper

freshly ground pepper

250 g small shrimp, cooked and shelled 1/2 lb

250 mL trimmed, washed and thinly
sliced fresh spinach 1 cup

125 mL crumbled feta cheese 1/2 cup

12 sheets of phyllo pastry 12

125 mL melted butter 1/2 cup

M E T H O D

1 Heat the olive oil in a large frying pan over
moderate heat and sauté the onion, garlic and
seasonings 3 to 5 minutes. Add the shrimp and
cook 2 minutes longer. Add the spinach, cook
1 minute and remove from heat. Let cool
completely.

2 Sprinkle with feta cheese and mix well.
Refrigerate until ready to use.

3 Preheat oven to 190ºC (375ºF).

4 To roll the treats, cut 1 sheet of phyllo pastry in
four, brush each piece with melted butter and
layer them. Place 30 mL (2 tbsp) of the shrimp
mixture in the centre and fold over.

5 Place the treats on a baking sheet and bake
15 minutes, or until golden brown. Serve
immediately.

6 These appetizers go well with a glass of ouzo.

Cod Balls

serves **4 to 6**

INGREDIENTS

500 g salt cod **1 lb**

1 clove garlic, chopped **1**

pinch cayenne pepper

freshly ground pepper

250 mL cold mashed potatoes **1 cup**

125 mL chopped fresh parsley **1/2 cup**

125 mL finely chopped onion **1/2 cup**

2 egg yolks **2**

250 mL flour **1 cup**

250 mL olive oil **1 cup**

250 mL Aioli (see recipe page 23) **1 cup**

M E T H O D

1   Place cod in a large bowl and cover with cold water. Let stand 12 hours, changing the water 6 to 8 times.

2   Remove the cod from the water and cut it into medium-sized pieces. Poach in hot water over very low heat 6 to 8 minutes. Drain well. Remove the skin and bones and let cool.

3   Shred the fish and place in a large bowl. Add the garlic, cayenne pepper, pepper, mashed potatoes, parsley, onion and egg yolks. Mix well. Moisten your hands and roll the mixture into balls. Coat the balls with flour, shaking off the excess.

4   Heat the olive oil in a large frying pan over high heat and brown the cod balls, a few at a time, 2 to 3 minutes. Drain on paper towels and serve hot or cold with Aioli.

Jamaican Frog Legs

serves **4 to 6**

INGREDIENTS

60 frog legs **60**

2 cloves garlic **2**

125 mL coarsely chopped green pepper **1/2 cup**

125 mL coarsely chopped green onion **1/2 cup**

1 mL crushed black peppercorns **1/4 tsp**

1 mL ground nutmeg **1/4 tsp**

2 mL ground allspice **1/2 tsp**

1 mL ground cinnamon **1/4 tsp**

1 bay leaf **1**

2 mL dried thyme **1/2 tsp**

2 mL ground coriander **1/2 tsp**

2 mL chopped fresh ginger **1/2 tsp**

60 mL olive oil **1/4 cup**

30 mL lime juice **2 tbsp**

1 chopped jalapeño pepper (optional) **1**

salt to taste

M E T H O D

1   Purée all the ingredients except the frog legs in a food processor 3 to 5 minutes.

2   Pour the mixture into a large bowl and add the frog legs. Toss gently. Marinate 1 hour in the refrigerator.

3   Grill the frog legs on a very hot barbecue or under a preheated broiler 3 to 5 minutes, or until the meat pulls away easily from the bones.

4   Serve immediately.

Creole Fried Squid

serves **4 to 6**

1 kg small squid, cleaned **2 lb**

250 mL milk **1 cup**

250 mL 35% cream **1 cup**

30 mL lemon juice **2 tbsp**

500 mL flour **2 cups**

30 mL paprika **2 tbsp**

30 mL onion powder **2 tbsp**

10 mL garlic powder **2 tsp**

10 mL ground cumin **2 tsp**

10 mL ground coriander **2 tsp**

2 mL ground nutmeg **1/2 tsp**

2 mL ground cloves **1/2 tsp**

1 mL cayenne pepper **1/4 tsp**

salt and freshly ground pepper

1 L peanut oil **4 cups**

Mango Dip

Mango Dip (makes 500 mL or 2 cups)

250 mL coarsely chopped mango **1 cup**

2 cloves garlic **2**

60 mL chopped green onion **1/4 cup**

60 mL chopped cilantro **1/4 cup**

10 mL Dijon mustard **2 tsp**

125 mL mango nectar **1/2 cup**

15 mL rice vinegar **1 tbsp**

30 mL olive oil **2 tbsp**

10 mL Worcestershire sauce **2 tsp**

pinch cayenne pepper

salt and freshly ground pepper

METHOD

1 Cut the bodies and tentacles of the squid into 0.5-cm (1/4-in.) strips. Set aside a few whole tentacles for the garnish. Place the squid in a large bowl and add the milk, cream and lemon juice. Mix well and marinate 1 hour in the refrigerator.

2 Combine the flour and seasonings in a large bowl. Let stand at room temperature until ready to use.

3 Drain the squid and coat in flour, shaking off the excess. Lower into very hot peanut oil (180°C / 350°F) 1 to 2 minutes. Drain well on paper towels.

4 Serve piping hot with Mango Dip.

MANGO DIP

1 Blend all the ingredients in a food processor or blender until creamy. Refrigerate until ready to serve.

Index